ROCOCO
and Other Worlds

WESLEYAN POETRY

A DRIFTLESS SERIES BOOK

This book is the 2010 selection in the Driftless Translation category, for a translation of poetry into English.

Afzal Ahmed Syed

ROCOCO
AND OTHER WORLDS

SELECTED POEMS

Translated from the Urdu by
Musharraf Ali Farooqi

WESLEYAN UNIVERSITY PRESS
Middletown, Connecticut

Published by
WESLEYAN UNIVERSITY PRESS
Middletown, CT 06459
www.wesleyan.edu/wespress

Manufactured in the
United States of America
5 4 3 2 1

The Driftless Series is funded by the
Beatrice Fox Auerbach Foundation Fund
at the Hartford Foundation for Public Giving.

Wesleyan University Press is a member of the Green Press Initiative. The paper used in this book meets their minimum requirement for recycled paper.

Originally published in Urdu by Aaj Ki Kitaben, Karachi: "An Arrogated Past" as *Chheeni Hoi Tareekh*, 1984; "Death Sentence in Two Languages" as *Do Zubanon Mein Saza-e Maut*, 1990; "Rococo and Other Worlds" as *Rokoko Aur Doosri Dunyaen*, 2000

Library of Congress Cataloging-in-Publication Data
Sayyid, Afzal Ahmad.
[Poems. English. Selections]
Rococo and other worlds: selected poems /
Afzal Ahmed Syed; translated from the Urdu by
Musharraf Ali Farooqi.
p. cm. — (Wesleyan poetry)
ISBN 978-0-8195-6933-2 (cloth: alk. paper)
I. Farooqi, Musharraf, 1968– II. Title.
PK2200.S3935A2 2010
891.4'39171—dc22 2009036032

This project is supported in part by an award from the National Endowment for the Arts.

CONTENTS

from Rococo and Other Worlds — 2000

from Death Sentence in Two Languages — 1990

from

ROCOCO
and Other Worlds

Rococo and Other Worlds

Elias Canetti maintains
Goya was a partisan
The one who made the Maja Nude
the Maja Clothed, and
the Majas on a Balcony

His Rococo world disappeared
in Third of May in a dark Madrid alley
He became oblivious
that parasol carriers had adorned his canvas and his bed

The source of light
in his canvas is a floor lantern
troops whose faces remain hidden
discharge fire on unresisting civilians
everyone resolves death in his own manner
the white shirt has his chest thrust out
in defiance
Successive generations of painters
shall revisit the theme

The subject of his last oil
the Milkmaid of Bordeaux
would have been claimed by some revolution

In the passing it may be mentioned
Goya sided against Napoleon
with the people of Spain

Viewers' Choice

Wandy D wants
to preserve our war against insects
for her viewers
(she will be compensated for her pains)

It is her good fortune
that at present we are targeted by locust swarms

She has
canceled her plans
to visit Ipanema or Copa Cabana
this summer
and the cut of the ultimate-bikini
is farthest from her thoughts

Armed with a printout
of possible hazards, diet and dress-code
she wants to take on
our psychedelic sun

The use of baking soda
as a teeth-whitener
is foreign to Doctor D
She is similarly disinterested
in a French manicure
(it is an expensive proposition!)

Locust swarms is what catches her fancy
documented by God, Pausanias and Pliny
From the vantage point of Etruscan emperors
she desires to see us fall in the arena

We desire
that Wandy should assume Farfara as her a.k.a.
have a part of her body temporarily or permanently tattooed
and perform
the bedroom act in some movie
that we could rent from the nearest video-library

A Difficult Question

Where was Cleopatra
at the time of Caesar's murder?

A free trip
to Rome
for one who solves the riddle

A Corroded Pin

Dr Pedro Ara
would have died of starvation
in our country
waiting for a commission
to embalm a corpse

To preserve their better halves
in flesh
after their tortuous deaths
occurred to none of our presidents

But not all presidents are alike
Nor all first ladies are prima-ballerinas
whom it does not behoove
to become earth again
if she breathes her last
as Dr Pedro Ara's compatriot
and the mistress of a head-of-state

In the presidential bedchamber
she lay in peace for three years
in her open casket

After his deposal
the former ruler shared with her his exile
and to reach a Madrid cellar
she forded the whole Atlantic

Three decades later
to reclaim power
the former president
again crossed the Atlantic
without the prima-ballerina's casket

For the simple reason that
his beloved –
the renowned actress –
had a revulsion for unsightly objects
such as
a corroded pin
in the hair of an embalmed corpse

The Spirit of the Lord

The Spirit of the Lord is moving over waters
over colorful waters
over twelve-year-vintage waters from Scotland
The Spirit of the Lord is speeding
dancing
doing somersaults
flinging its arms wide
blowing kisses
to pull together
someone who must stand for his master
in the morning
to inaugurate a by-pass bridge

The Inaugural Plaque Is Stolen

The plaque worth
one thousand US dollars
installed at a project's inauguration
has been stolen
It is no trifling matter
One must not sit still
after lodging an FIR against unknown thieves
Islamabad must dispatch
five-thousand-strong Police and Rangers detachments
to surround the area
conduct house-to-house searches
carry out arrests of youth
shower children with slaps
strike white heads against walls
snatch anything that takes their fancy

In the event the plaque's not recovered
the guard
that did not search the black Mercedes
of the guest-of-honor on his way out
should be dismissed

Spring Shall Return to the City

By virtue of the prime minister's
photogenic smile
Adonis-like
the murdered youth shall return from Hades
and other victims too

The president shall clear his throat
and the terrorists will surrender arms
and get jobs at the Mehran Bank

In the afternoon
the moment the Chief Minister's yawn is ended
the citizenry shall set out for movie houses and theaters
Topless nymphomaniac girls will come out to the French Beach

The moment our eyes pop and the tongues loll out
from bodies strung up
on boughs of trees
Spring shall return to the city

It Could Never Be

Her love
for haute-couture
Her embroidered bolero
Her Egyptian amulet for eternal life
Her partiality
towards Islam and chocolate-chip ice cream
Her bridal gown, and for swearing-in ceremonies her green
    and her blue dresses
People ordered stripped at her behest
it could never be

The Campaign to Introduce an Ice-Cream

After the Rangers trucks
and the armored personnel carriers
before the tanks made an appearance
they rolled out of toy shops
into our streets
with their white boxes-on-wheels
fitted out with beach-umbrellas

They spoke the language of strawberry and vanilla
To attract people
they had a charming tune

Their campaign
to introduce an ice-cream
was the last pleasant surprise for our city

A Girl

Her moans
in the throes of ecstasy
sound more melodious
than the whole world's national anthems

During the sexual act
she could be determined more pretty
than any beauty queen

A visit to any strife torn part of the city
could be risked
to obtain
her blue video

Only to meet her
is impossible
Like Pakistan
Hala Faruqi too
is in police custody

On a Political Party Being Allotted the Horse as Its Election Symbol

Do not appear on a wretched piece of paper; do not conceal Odysseus and his wily companions in your belly; walk out of the posters smeared on Aabpara walls and trot neighing past Constitution Avenue; get under the Amazons' thighs; unseat Nelson at the Trafalgar; head straight for Giambologna's studio and walk in without knocking; take al-Mutanabbi to the Sultan's tent — for the first time in history a poet will read out his *qasida* astride a horse; come out of the bank lockers; break the vaults, and Samson-like bring down the pillars of the head office; do not submit your mane to the lawn mower; Eve is presenting Adam an apple bought from the supermarket, pluck it from her hands and present it to your favorite filly; go aboard and discover the America that Isabella could not buy for all her crown jewels; enslave Alexander and Julius Caesar; pull Adonis's bier to its last resting place; locate sunken ships; search for the Earth's treasures; invent a new variety of grass; wear the moon as a stud in your shoe; do not look back at the Minotaur; Jesus doesn't have a ride, take him to Mary Magdalene's place this evening under falling showers; Nefertiti has never set eyes on a horse, imagining you the God she will prostrate herself before you; do not let your flanks be branded; do not let your image be stamped.

Britannicus

On the eve of Saturnalia
his melancholy strains
had stirred the drunken mob

But words failed him then
his spasms on the white alabaster floor
soon ended

He shall never again roll dice against his elder brother

"He shall come to soon enough!"
Nero declared with imperial fluency
The mother of the murderer and his victim
had lost all
He had been poisoned before everyone's eyes
to the right of the holy relics

He died
without giving his sister a farewell kiss
and lay thus in the banquet hall
After a brief silence
everyone dug into their food again

Astronomy and the Poet

As an homage to love, the volcano of a Martian moon was named after the beloved of the man who had discovered that moon and another, whose naming after a mythical god was influenced by the worship instinct — a lesser passion than love. But we can overlook that as the god in question was killed. What affords us satisfaction is that a satellite of Mars was baptized after the one who made the first unsuccessful flight, and that to invest the cosmos with some semblance of purpose, at least the regions of Mercury were named after a poet, a novelist, a painter, and a composer. Aphrodite, the deity of love, reigns over just one region of Venus, whereas Satellite No. 433 was determined as the God of Fornication. The satellite named after the God Hermes was unfortunately lost after it drew one thousand meters too close to Earth. Those who venerate wealth would be delighted to learn that the goddess of the Roman mint is in revolution as a Martian satellite. All the illustrious cosmic gods whose worshipers became extinct or were put to the sword, are in orbit somewhere or the other, with their august names. Some day someone will also name a planetoid — discovered somewhere in the far reaches of the space — after our God.

A Beginning with Great Names

We do not at all know
where Alice Rendal may be found at this hour
This past day she was seen at the hotel pool's western side
and in the telescope
of Godhra Camp's Ibrahim Borka
on the Industrial Corporation's fifth floor

Were he a silkworm
he would have woven a cocoon around her
and the two would have been dropped in boiling water together

Our sympathies and our nights
go out to the girls
who saw off their childhood speedily and with insolence
Our love
goes out to the girl
whose eyes tell New York time
whose nail polish glows in the dark
She is actively trying to save the race of dolphins

The best of all nights
was spent in her permed hair
We were at variance over Germany's reunification

Yet we know
the heart is a trapeze artist
that keeps up its act
without an audience

Wellai Wang-Ik
is lying stripped and joyful in her room
and could entertain guests in that state
but our knowledge is short

Beginning today
we must
call the two girls Helen and Beatrice —
who pass by Mansfield Street
at half past five in the evening —
that we may make a beginning with two great names

A Dog's Death

Air Vice-Marshal Manocher Nadirshaw
taking his dinner
during a civilian flight
chokes on a bone
and dies

Throw another dog
before just such a bone

Tell Me a Story

Tell me a story
other than that you're carrying my seed
other than that you're more beautiful
than the girl who has left me
other than that you always wear a white brassiere
under a white blouse

Tell me a story
other than who the mirror pronounced the loveliest
other than that all reflection in the mirror is beautiful
other than how the princesses' mirrors
slipped from the slave-girls' hands
other than how the princesses' fetuses aborted
other than how the cities fell
                    and the ramparts
                    and the standards
                    and men in combat

Tell me a story
other than that you did not sleep in the Captain's cabin
sailing over the dateline
other than that you never set eyes on the sea
other than that of the drowned
some names never make the list

Tell me a story
other than how in a brothel separated twin sisters met
other than what flower grew from whose tears
other than that from a burning oven nobody steals bread

Tell me a story
other than how from the museum
the witness table of the peace pact disappeared
other than that a continent is called by the wrong name

Tell me a story
other than that you do not like to kiss lips
other than that I was not the first man in your life
other than that it was not raining that day

Soldiers Seize Virgil's Lands

Soldiers seize Virgil's lands
whose restoration lies
a journey to Rome and two poems
farther on

The length of his stay there
and how long the civil war detained him
from writing poetry
remains unrecorded

From his Spanish campaign
Emperor Augustus
sends for
the manuscript of the Aeneid
which was read to him four years later
on his deathbed

Virgil repeatedly sent for the manuscript of the Aeneid —
to destroy it —
it was not provided him

The Ultimate Profession

It is common knowledge that the ultimate profession is to earn one's bread through plying the pen. Recently cradle-makers and fossilologists have also shown an inclination towards this calling, and in this line of work every deposed general has attained an enviable rank. Ousted bureaucrats and murderers condemned for life are the authors of best-selling books. We make the sad observation that in the opinion of her contemporaries, Aphra Behn—the first woman who sought recourse to penmanship to earn bread—earned her living, principally, from selling her flesh.

from

DEATH SENTENCE in Two Languages

If My Voice Is Not Reaching You

If my voice is not reaching you
add to it the echo —
echo of ancient epics

And to that —
a princess

And to the princess—your beauty

And to your beauty —
a lover's heart

And in the lover's heart
a dagger

The Last Date of Existence

Our breathing follows
no distinct tune
And our blood
could easily be washed with liquid soap
Without prior sanction we could change the color
of our raincoat or footwear
We are not admonished
presenting a girl with a taper-holder —
or a schooner —
in our dream
On the empty steps of the winding staircase
we are allowed the privilege
to await a kiss

The last date of our existence is expired

You Live in Lovely Orbs

You live in lovely orbs
A sphericality
conscientiously
holds your hair

An ornate necklace
truckles your neck

The unfaltering watch
is attached to your wrist

A dainty belt
embraces your waist

Your feet are girdled
in lace-up
shoes to tread our earth

I shall not mention the hidden orbs
that might have you in their hold
Allow them the advantage
that is theirs

In my mind in play
I never disarrayed you

You live in lovely orbs
And I in tortuous lines
How may I possibly serve you
except
fetch you in my mouth the ball
you kicked

Poem

You arrive
daily decked out in a new outfit
to teach your alluring eyes
a new language

Between your lowered neck
and your shoulder
I find a new clasp
for my heart

Looking out the window
your eyes
rest on my face

Pronouncing the unfamiliar phrase
my tongue is caught
between your teeth

Through the window
perhaps
we could walk far
towards the sea
ignoring the throng of scrap mongers
scrapping a ship

Perhaps we could cross over the bridge
that has been condemned
Sit in benches
where the paint has not dried

Zarmeena

Zarmeena whom it was given me to discover with the compass and the astrolabe, addressed me in three languages, and also in an aquatic language yet to be contrived. At the Promulgation of the Canon of Nature's Mimicry prohibiting food and drink, the schedules of manufactories and lyceums had been revised, and Zarmeena, who would not have cared much for the discrepancies on the terrestrial domain, loyal to the old calendar, reached the lyceum at a time when the books and the walls had all been locked. I had not left the lyceum that day. I was on the verge of being locked inside when I saw her and she returned me my collection of poems. Oblivious of myself, when handing her the book, I could not, in either language, present it to her. Even so, she relied on my pledge of the Aquatic God and kept it in her custody: she unfolded several poems and chanced to learn from history that poets were not loved; and that it was still difficult for one whose heart and star were made with water. But her eyes, which require no preface, could not desist from the question that if her boat would best others on the First Morn, would I dedicate to her my new collection of verse, keeping in view that she had disclosed to me the place from which the sea looked its most beautiful and where after bribing the guards I had spent a whole day. Zarmeena was not there that day. She did not wish my love of the sea apportioned. She was not there another day when I went to look her up in the holds of boats, and where the seamen eat. Even so, when she was turned out innocent from the bibliothèque, to console her I was there; within the walls of the painting exhibit I was locked with her and freed. The last time I walked away from her, she came with her carriage and found it most improper not to see me home. But she knew nothing of the garden of caged beasts and the heart of the city, adjacent. So she could have dropped me at will, anywhere. Before we could cross the bridge that separates mirth from sorrow in my city, she asked me a few questions, which everyone sooner or later asks, who would enter or break a relationship. Deciding not to take her too deep into the recesses of sorrow, without caring to ask when or where I next might see her, I asked to be dropped at the foot of the bridge. I never saw her again. Incessantly I searched for her at the steps of the Admiralty, near shops that sell sails, and in auberges near the sea. The blue ink that smeared her wrist one day during the lesson would keep reminding me I could have gathered her in a poem.

Zarmeena, if she is too near the sea, must needs feel obligated to me—for I could well have distanced her from the sea with the magnet's help.

The Genres of Poetry

Without knowing that nomadism is a creed of life and among poetry's more difficult genres, he found his way to a tattered amphitheatre and began to dream of tightrope walkers; but his ropes were not yet woven when a non-nomad girl appeared before him who took him many light-years away from nomadism. This encounter exposed him to the shadow of light and blood and in a bird shop he priced the dream of a fledgling of exquisite plumage in maiden flight, until the spool of his voice flew away from his hands. The custodian of the bird shop pasted him to the wall of an edifice and from there, in exchange for cartage and a time-and-a-half allowance, he was taken to a cell where someone addressed him. The liveliest drop of blood in his body which sometimes disrobes in his eyes, is the voice of the girl he heard, and found out that the paper blossoms, the glass vase, the brick wall, the wooden door, and even he himself, could speak, in the accent and language of his choice. He did not see the girl but like the lighthouse which the waves perhaps never reach, he saw how the sea lay, and the parts where it was turbulent. The live drop of blood which once answered to his fingers disappeared in his body of a sudden. From that moment he turned bitter, and now searched for an adversary. Ages later it dawned on him that both friend and foe are terms for a lost blessing. But for now he had no patience and set forth the charges against his father in his verses. This self-instilled enmity which solidified one day, allowed him to search in his father's eyes for the face of the girl he could pronounce mother, or not pronounce it. Around that time he was granted bail from the prison that was his home. Those who bailed him out introduced him to the pack of fifty-two fairies. The training in self-denial and his suicidal tendency brought out in him a gambler's keenness. He gambled excessively but could not forfeit himself. Then he played a strange trick, becoming partners with a preceptress in life. The drop of blood that disrobed in his eyes was absorbed in the preceptress's white chalk. After some time, one day when she drew a fledgling in maiden flight, the picture flew away from the blackboard. When he learnt of the incident, he began to dream of nomad girls who can walk on air without tightropes—without knowing that this variety of nomadism is poetry's most complex genre.

To Live Is a Mechanistic Torture

To live is a mechanistic torture
We can realize why
girls who commit suicide
cutting open their vaginas
leave no farewell note

And how
the bones of children flex
Like a tree's green bough

This tree is native to Pakistan

We know
on which banquet table
our national colors are polishing apples
However,
of witnesses there are four categories
and the verdict is always legibly penned

We cannot be likened to the girl
who does not know what it means to give consent
And is loath to kiss
the queen's black brassieres
and her three thousand shoes

The poison administered us
shall not be expelled from our body through tears

Looking through the venetian blind
we could see
how the sea wolves
are impregnating our women
and where
our equations are being solved

Still it lies on us
to inform
the man
trying to pull out with his finger tips
the invisible thread
that to live is also a phantasmal torture

I Was Taken with an Indigo Flower

I was taken with an indigo flower. By that I allude to the girl I loved. I could also say her name but the world is crowded with people. I had met her on the twin bridges far away from my home that were inadvertently built side by side over a lake. Sometimes we would walk over a bridge together and sometimes over our separate bridges hold each other's hands. With my first wages I bought nails and between fixing the loosened planks of the bridge and composing a verse for her eyes, hammered a nail into the palm of my hand and realized I was not made of wood. In an internecine war perhaps that bridge was torched. I could never buy nails for another bridge again.

Whom One Loves

Whom one loves
must be conducted
out
of a fading city
on the last boat

With the beloved
one must cross over
a bridge
condemned to be razed

The syllables in a beloved name must always be softened

The beloved must be shown around
an isle
abounding in live volcanoes

The beloved
must be first kissed
inside
a torture cell
in a salt mine

With the beloved
one must type
a memorandum
against all inequities in the world
whose pages
one must fling
out the hotel window
towards the swimming pool
come morning

The Last Contention

Your love
demands greater justice than before
It showered in the morning
which saddens you
This sight had the right to be immortalized
The memory of a besieged heart did not trouble you
opening this window on the verdant expanse

Over a nameless bridge
you told yourself in a firm voice
I shall keep alone

You did not consider love
a startling fortune

My luck was not made in a shipyard
yet I forded the lengths of sea
kept mysteriously alive
and relentlessly wrote poetry

I profess to have all the faults
of a lover
and the last contention

Has Love Been Mislaid

Was your dress
never lowered for love
or your heart
never raised into air with doves
from bedecked balconies?

I watched the dance from a distance
and the danseuse up close
worn-out she could have sought my arms to sleep in
but she could not outpace her heart

For a long while
I felt your presence in the seat adjacent

Is my heart an empty seat
whose ticket you have mislaid?
Has love been mislaid?

We built an ornamental fireplace
in our room
and met each other
like strangers

On the day of the flower exhibit
you walked away
without a parting kiss

It was raining outside

An umbrella remained furled up in my heart

Had We Not Sung the Song

We know
how meaningful
is the life
we live

We know
the mass of stones
that from our neglect
turned into things
whose beauty
our lives did not advance

That moment
we felt
our hearts
among the flowers put on the altar
as we walked in the parade
of wounded horses

Defeat is our God
We shall worship him in our deaths
We shall die the death
of a man in agony

Life would never have reckoned
what we sought of it
had we not sung the song

Poem

Every day
I fall in love with you anew
The capital was in the grip of autumn
And in the frozen boulevard I was wandering
holding your hand
kissing you at every turn
In the hotel suite
under the apple-green blanket
you were together with me
It was altogether you
to whom I was reading
the poems of my favorite poet
when the shades of night were falling

Love

To your feet
my heart
is as the bridge
whose walk was inundated

I fell from favor
like the dog
who could not tell his name to the new owner
and his previous master has died in some accident

I failed myself
in securing me a miserable death
and in composing an obscene lay
that instead of the white kerchief
you could have used to dry a teardrop

Ashes fill up my shoes
and my feet are missing

Love is not a standard
nor arms nor an oath
to be lightly assumed

Ashes fill up my heart
and a foreign toxin
Love is a snare
filled up with ashes
and my two hands

I wasted myself
in wait of showers
that would wash away
my feet, my heart and my hands
that you might make of them a memorial
and call it love

A Parable

He had a firm hold on this sensation that it was daybreak. He turned in bed. This movement was in itself very gentle as his feelings were never devoid of the regard for the planks of the bed that could not withstand negligence and would dislocate from the frame. The rays of sunlight were piercing him, as if the sun, which belongs to nomads and charioteers all, and which for sundry considerations no one now calls God, was about to raise him on the lances of its rays. The same rays were also smarting his eyes, and for this very reason he had a firm hold on the event of the break of day, and for the selfsame reason he could not let go of the sensation of the loss of his sight. He could not see a thing, and it was morning.

The listeners to this tale, by virtue of their altruistic nature or benevolence, might perhaps be expectant that further down, by error or through a miracle, the sight of the man will be restored, which is erroneous.

When the man had no pretext left to refute the fact of the loss of his sight—for darkness is its own contention—he must have tried to make much ado: the usual reactions of a man during or after a calamity: crying, yelling, flailing arms about, turning away from God and resolving on suicide. Men who are not written about in stories take forever to get through these stages, but he lived them all in a flash, and then he again turned extremely gently in the bed, because after all the planks of his bed were vulnerable to disregard, and on the bed within his reach slept the woman who was impregnated with his sight. He wished to reveal his situation to the woman, but left himself to be discovered. The woman is close to awakening; it is morning after all.

As he had wished, the loss of his sight became apparent to his woman, became apparent to his neighbors, his kin, friends and acquaintances, his juniors, his superiors, all, and if he had had a mother it would have become apparent to her too. Then things took their usual course. He was retired from his position with a modest stipend, and his woman found employment.

Then one day he told his woman that he wished to change the house. The house was changed. After a long time it dawned on the woman that he could not climb stairs from memory, that he had lost count.

His woman, the fact of whose pregnancy has been detailed, one day gave birth to a girl. On the occasion the man was as overwhelmed with happiness as any father capable of regarding his daughter. After a long time he felt the contention of darkness being refuted. His daughter had light in both her eyes.

He continued in his efforts to discern his daughter's features by fondling her face with his fingertips when someone told him of her likeness to him, and on learning that, he was delighted. At that moment he thought of what his features were like, and the same moment realized that his face had been lost to him. He pondered for days and was continuously disappointed. His woman, neighbors, friends, kin, he entreated them all for the recovery of his features; many a memory that had been prevented from stirring went crazy, but despite all he could not recall his face, and now only a miracle could restore it to him. The reason for his continuing belief in miracles is beyond the comprehension of the storyteller.

Often, when his woman was absent, he wished to strangle his daughter so that no one could remind him of their resemblance. But he could not rationalize such audacity with logic.

In a small house by the sea a change came to his life. A girl whom he might have loved in adolescence came to know of his condition, and one day she graced a small house by the sea with her man and children. The same day his woman and the other woman's man observed the miraculous likeness of the other woman's children to the man whose story is not yet ended. This observation was ignored with as much ceremony as the surprise with which it had been made. Then on some festive occasion the other woman's man, on behalf of himself and his woman, presented the sightless man with a dog. Sooner or later everyone who has lost his sight finds himself with a dog. He named the dog after himself.

Then he took such courage that he roamed the seaside with the dog, and returned home in the evening to a waiting woman holding a girl's hand.

The narrator of this story cannot tell whether all continued as before, or his sea inundated the townships, or his dog reverted, or his wife, or daughter, or both, became depraved, ran away from home, or died. A story narrated with pen and ink must be considered told where it is ended.

Near Lavania

There, where silence lies flanked by armed sentinels, with her I call the bread, the bread and the wine, the wine. With her verdant fingers she touches an aquatic bell and dead horsemen rush galloping past under the boughs of the flower-of-the-unknown-name. She says that in the rain the flower a man gives a woman always carries the same meaning. Hope, which disarrays our night and our day, brings her to the black juniper tree. The name of this land is Genesis. Where we shall be picked with the vines and brewed, there I present to her a horse, and to me she gives an olive plant—the one made of glass and naphtha and wood and stone and wool.

Near Lavania, I touch her flower bearing five wounds and closing the puerto morona kiss her lips. I am the weed which grows outside the stable; a tablet with plaintive letters; the loneliest fish in the net; the memory of a heartsick princess; an Argonaut forsaken back on land.

In flight we taste many seasons, and now it's snowing heavily, and I cover her wholly with flowers. The moon is in Virgo. The bricks of this building were laid in the full moon. In those days I was living dangerously and except for the dream I had no word.

Could her wide blue eyes be more erroneously read?

Those Who Own the Filly

Pedigree mares are mated
at the time of year when flowers bloom
In autumn they run on wagers

A wooden horse
soon to be sawn apart
for a petty sum
shall mate with
the Queen of Fortune
Odysseus and his warriors
will be cut to pieces

History is a document of coming into heat of mares
who, had they not been mated,
would have reduced all race-courses
to fields covered with burnt grass

In an effort to flow with the tide of History
a stallion
is mounting a quivering spot
clasped in the depth
is faking an orgasm
without removing his lunettes —
leaping into a thought —
is taking the hit on his sex

With the pair of jaws
catching tight to the mane
making love to the filly
who could not wait for the historian's fingers
to probe her ovaries

The crazed horse
cannot understand that
the breeders —
those who own the filly —
without making a wager on their mark
shall shoot him
the moment he withdraws
after making love

A Couplet by Poet-Laureate Nubar Isbarian

The beauty of the couplet that poet-laureate Nubar Isbarian composed for his courtesan Irma's breasts would be lost in translation as Irma's breasts were wasted on the sands of River Esta. In Armenia it surpassed the acclaim accorded the couplets that Nubar Isbarian had written for his beloved and contemporary poetess, Nura Na'albandian's eyes, that were cited as the epitome of the highest poetry. Poetess Nura Na'albandian was so tormented by the couplet that oftentimes she was disposed to put out her eyes with the gift dagger from her former lover, goldsmith Jaraer Sambarian, which she was only permitted to put in her heart. The couplet earned such renown in the length and breadth of Armenia that every woman—from women of easy virtue to chaste virgins—even the cloistered nuns of the Convent of Turikian, entreated Nubar Isbarian, declaring they would bare their breasts for him if he would compose for them as elegant a couplet or even one that was somewhat inferior. Troubled by the celebrity of the couplet, the annalists regularly reported that Nubar Isbarian had never seen Irma's breasts bare, nor felt them with his hands, for to make such poetry about a thing seen or felt was beyond human capacity. Irma was aware of these reports, and also of the apple-orchard that she had cost Nubar Isbarian. And also, that Nubar Isbarian, under the spell of her breasts or antagonized by the annalists, is abdicating his vocation. Before it could have been reported in future chronicles that poet-laureate Nubar Isbarian had stopped writing poetry, with the holy dagger in goddess Ardvazi's temple, Irma severed her breasts and threw them on the sands of River Esta.

Step into My Parlor

Step into my Parlor,
death says to me

In her person
I see my beloved
undressed
identify my ejaculation
flowing on her thighs
she carries the foetus of the poem
I could not write —
carries a snare
I aimed at a star

Step into my Parlor,
death says to me
not knowing
that now I have nothing to give her

Poem

When the vanquished women of Yanieh
were singing of a new love in their songs

In indigo looted from Sidon
when the headmen
were dyeing the corpses

When the citizens of Nish
saw the birds fettered in brass chains
flying away in pairs

When a youth
emerged from the well of Aama
wielding a golden oar
and without identifying himself
fell dead

Of wheatish breasts
the deep-naveled Mehrema
without waiting for the snow to melt
came to me astride the mare
whose eyes had been put out
and gave me the hourglass
filled with black sand

In the temple of Artemis
that went up in flames
the day after
we made the last adoration
Before every blood stained taper-holder
I kissed her lips

From its lips, my severed head brought before Wasil
suddenly spurted blood
and the beautiful Mehrema
withdrew from Wasil's side

I Was Not Born to This Destiny

I was not born in the month of making verses; nor spotless white horses were pulling this century. To celebrate my coming into existence a bowl of starch must have been distributed among neighbors who no longer solemnized the festival of blooming verdure. My first friend must have been the mynah who repeated her name to me, and under one roof in separate cages we were both imprisoned. There were not one or more columns in front of our house. No kind or flint-hearted woman was appointed my nanny who would have covered me or some wounded animal with garlands. My father had no ivory cane to beat me with. My mother would have become renowned for her long hair and long poems had my father not cut them off with his sickle.

I was thrown on the fish nets that were laid away after the river silted up. The first thing my teeth felt must have been the wooden trough filled with the vomit of dogs. Quite early I must have learnt to fill my stomach with wild barley and the blood-red rice that was never among the food placed in the lake as offering for the dead.

The peace pact was being witnessed when my father tendered his resignation from life, and knowing full well that no one else would have found the sea more compassionate, I pledged to carry out my plan to ford channels and straits; but my mother knew that I was not born to die anonymous on a faraway isle. Announcing my death as she covers me with a blood-stained sheet, she will recognize that I never lost a war.

from An ARROGATED Past

I Invented Poetry

The Moroccans invented the papyrus
the Phoenicians, the alphabet
I invented Poetry

The grave-digger invented the oven
Those who appropriated the oven invented the bread ticket
The bread eaters invented the queue
and learned the chorus

With ants joining the bread-queue
Starvation was invented

The mulberry-seller invented the silkworm
With silk, poetry made the girls' wardrobe
For girls dressed in silk, the procuress invented the palace
where they betrayed the silkworm's domicile

Distance invented the galloping charger
Speed, the chariot
And when defeat was invented
I was thrown in front of the speeding chariot

But by that time poetry had invented love

Love invented the heart
The heart made tent and canoes
and traversed far-off lands

The eunuch invented the fish-hook
and slipped away piercing it in the slumbering heart
To catch the line to which the heart was snared
Auction was invented
And tyranny invented the final bid

I bartered the whole of poetry for fire
and burnt the Tyrant's hand

The Clay-mine

I work in a clay-mine
we are searched after work
our guards dislocate our every joint
Then we are put together
our guards do it callously;

The first day of work instead of my own
I was implanted with someone else's part
And it goes on and on
until every single strand
has been relocated
Who knows
of those grafted to my miscellaneous parts
how many have died in mine-collapses
for stealing clay
immolated

Inside the clay-mine several items are proscribed
In the clay-mine water is prohibited
Water washes away the clay along with its authority

If the guards realize
we had had water before setting foot in the mine
we are put in the vice
and every last drop of water squeezed out
And for every drop of water recovered
a day's wage lost

In the clay-mine fire blazes unbounded
No guards set limits on fire
Fire walls demarcate different sectors of the mine

I also labor between the four walls of fire
no labor could be performed without

In the clay-mine fire serves another end
Sometimes when the guards must suddenly vacate the mine
It is filled with fire
That day if one could get away with one's life
One is not searched
That day alone could clay be stolen

I had stolen the clay one such day

I have put away that clay
One other such day when the fire was being pumped
I had stolen from the pile of useless parts
my nails and heart-line
and put them away too

Of such fires somehow I am always abreast
and on the lookout

I have spotted a leg on the refuse pile
which is not mine
but, nevertheless, shapely
At the next fire I shall carry it away
And something else after that—and after that something else

One day I shall construct of my choice a whole man

I am anxious about that whole man
who shall be completed one day
and will not work in the clay-mine

I shall steal clay for him
And will research
how the mine is set on fire
Shall set it afire
and steal clay

Enough clay for the man
to have a house, an urn to store water in, and a lamp

And shall steal fire for the lamp
Fire is not something you steal
But as needs grow one could steal anything

Then that man could endure to live with me
If one has a house, a store of water to drink from, and a lamp
One could put up with anyone
I shall invite him to break bread with me
and if the bread was short
I'd steal bread
Not that the guards grudge their leftovers
to laborers who do not cause stir in the mine

I never spoke a word inside the clay-mine
nor without
I shall teach my whole man my language
and converse with him

I shall not discuss with him the clay-mine
I do not approve of people discussing work at home

I shall talk to him
about voyages of deep-seas

And if I could steal, and implant him with a throbbing heart
I shall talk with him of love
Of the girl whom I loved
Of the girl whom he shall love

I shall not keep him forever
No one could keep anyone forever
I shall encourage him to travel
and send him to the region
where trees grow out of the earth without rain

And he shall bring for me the seeds
to burgeon
that do not need moisture

Each day a seed
I shall sow in the clay-mine
Shall keep sowing
One day a season comes when a seed must sprout

In the clay-mine the seed sown by me shall germinate
and the plant sprout

My guards shall be greatly alarmed
They have never seen a tree
Greatly distressed, they shall take flight

Noticing a guard flee
I shall follow him to the other exit of the mine
with its exits exposed a mine holds no terrors

With my dread exorcised
I shall cross the walls of fire
and survey the mine to its far ends
and in a deserted corner
tunnel up

The tunnel shall be dug
right underneath

Where a river flows

I want a river

I am the one who sold his river
to buy a bridge
and wished to subsist
on the toll thereof
But no one ever crossed the riverless bridge

I sold the bridge
and bought a boat
but a riverless boat got no fare

I sold the boat
and bought a strong net
But the riverless net was cast in vain

I sold the net
and bought a parasol
And sold shade to travelers over the riverless land

By slow degrees
the travelers stopped coming

One day when
the shade of the sun fell short of my parasol's
I sold the parasol
and bought some bread

In any trade this is the last commerce

After a night
or after some nights
when nothing was left of the bread
I found an employ

I found the employ in the clay-mine

I Was Not Given Life in Such Plenitude

I was not given life in such plenitude
My rivers always reached me through the adversary's ranks
I always drank others' leftover dregs
I had to leave a season empty for the rains
The one who mentioned me in his will
never went barefoot in the rains

I do not know whether
he's the same
with him in her arms whose mother begged mercy of horsemen
and all her living days
who kept turning her face from the horse's steaming nostrils
I do not know whether
he's the same
whose mother had bound him in the cradle

From my mother's arms
and my cradle I would continually fall
Because I was born in a well
which never saw water
and began living in a house

Made with the broken rafters of a boat

I made a boat of reeds
and rowed it with stone oars

On the desolate shore of her city
I sowed a crop
and harvested one

The ivory moon
stands guard on lilies
Her jars of wax and honey she guards

Who is to tell
if the ivory moon in my sky as well she hadn't discovered
like the North Star she did for me
and had the old canal dug

I know
how her father
transforms from a trinket-peddler into a tradesman
how
in the ballroom on my way to ask her for a dance I
join the queue before charity-givers
blowing on the horn

Though
I am the one
on wet steps who
is for blocking the sun's way —
even on the day
when those who see fire turn to stone

To the vat if the grapes are transferred from the vine
Her valleys are not sapped
Their wool not shorn
Say to her that
To some irate god a prisoner was sacrificed

And
It was the time
When mothers throw their first-born
in front of racing chariots
that I was brought into a burnt city

Admirable are the cities
in the name of girls founded, that are burnt in the name of gods
Admirable are the girls
in hands sticking out of ripped graves
who lay the first pick of the fruits

If poetry could save love
With my poetry I'd have joined the two ends of the sea

But with the pardon in my hand
the functionaries of her god
are demolishing my sanctuary

Could this sea be my exile?
That would assure me
So long as I shall remain on its shores
I will exist as son of man

Who knows when that ship would sink anchor
whose skipper would light a fire for me

Who knows when
the patron goddess of this city
shall grant me her blessing
in that I did not make the ranks
who marked one lone night in her caravanserais

Without supplication when
an apple begets fragrance
And a serpent, venom
without anathema
With some burnt metropolis' stones when
a new city is being founded
To my land may I return

This sea shall retreat
and inundate the townships
In the tradition of the seas

Only one woman would survive in her city —
that would be her
And one eunuch would survive in her city —
that could be anyone

Perhaps
her heart
of any mulberry tree is bereft
My heart though
is a silkworm
I have rid my identity of this worm
And along with it
I creep

"The one not with me
now stands against me"

If Someone Would Remember Me

The winter is here
And so is the proclamation to provide prisoners with woolen
  blankets

The nights have changed,
their length, their breadth and their weight
But every night I dream
of being held slipping the fence

During the change in weather
In the time that escapes measurement
I read a poem

My brother wrote it as he left for the front
From where he was not returned alive

But I intend—being more conscientious than he—
to live the full term of my life

I realize that
The machines are dry
That dogs are going without rations

I realize that
Snow and the clouds are most innocent
And mountains
Most strong
I realize that
Those who live in the mountains
Are most poor
That winters make them further destitute

Nothing much in rains could be written on the walls
But now that winter's come
If someone would remember me —
Like the girl
reading my poems who breaks into tears —
Something regarding my freedom could be written on the walls

I realize that
My poems shall remain under hearing
I realize that
to bail my heart —
prisoner of a wall and floor far colder than these —
nobody would come

I realize that
Before everyone gets his woolen blanket
the winter would have passed

What the Sea Said to You

"What did the sea tell you?"
The prosecution lawyer asks you
and you break out in tears

"Your Honor! The question is irrelevant!"
The defense objects, wiping your tears

The court overrules the objection
and your tears

The tears are put away in the record room
and you in your cell

This city lies below the sea-level
These courts below the city's
and the cells of the accused on trial
still further down

In your cell someone hands you a silk yarn
From appearance to appearance you spin a shawl
Unraveling it
after the court is adjourned

"How did you come into possession of this yarn?"
the superintendent of prisons asks you

"A man brought this yarn
tied to his feet
To slay a monster
To find his way out of the labyrinthine pass"

"Whereabouts is that man now?"
You are ducked in cold water and asked

"The man has lost his way!"
That was what the sea had told you

If They Could Learn

If they could learn
the way to kill us

They harass life
bribe death,
and blindfold it

They send us gifts of scimitars
hoping
they we would waste ourselves

In the zoo, they
keep the netting in the lion's enclosure vulnerable
And the day we visit
take the lion off its rations
When the moon's not broken in fragments
They invite us to visit an isle
And the paper guaranteeing our lives there
In the boat they mislay

If they could learn
That they are poor assassins
They would break out in a sweat
and be deprived of their job

They dream of our dying
and burn all books of interpretations

They make vaults in our name
and bury their booty within

Even learning
of the way to kill us

They could hardly kill us

To Live Another Day

On a far-away shore
On a ship made of scrap
The boiler explodes

The Second Engineer dies the same day
The Third Engineer, the next

And I
The Fourth Engineer
Die on the third

No First Engineers are assigned
to second-hand ships
Or else
I'd have lived another day

If I Do Not Return

I snare blind cheetahs
colored fish
flying clouds

Blind cheetahs are snared
in traps dug with dull pickaxes
colored fish
in silk-strung nets
and flying clouds
with magnets

This is my well
This, my oven
and this, my grave
I have dug them all

The one who must cut his fetters himself
Must needs grow his own file
I must part my sea myself
My boat I shall myself obtain
The painted boat that is drying on a shore or
stopped in a cave or
imprisoned in a tree or
is nowhere

But I have a seed
called my heart
I have a little land
called love

I shall grow a tree of my heart
One day
Of that I shall make a boat
And set sail

If I do not return
Put my colored fish in my well
my blind cheetahs
in my oven
and my flying clouds
in my grave

That I have made deep

The Slaughter of Snow-Birds

This is the story of the slaughter of snow-birds
But I shall begin it from your body

Your body was wild barley
That was sold, robbed or ravaged

The dress woven of ibex wool and cedar fiber
I wore the day I took oath —
on the rawhide shield and the magnetic-ring in your finger —
of life

In cupped mirrors
was an image of variegated sands

"It's me!"
you said
and the mirrors began to cloud

Your supplication in the world's most ancient tongue
was received
Both as a song and a lie
I only wish you had not kindled your body so

Preceding God's Day of Fire
was the Day of our Union

At harvest time of the quick-growing crop
the images of an alien god
were polluting waters

When I relinquished a dream
and saw a part of my life
coalescing in water

The cemetery gates
were painted red with vermilion
And the way further up was strewn
with common pearls
and fish-hooks made of bone
Other than your body I had no net
to rescue the sinking life

I said to you
Give me two locks of your hair
and help mother weave them into a bow-string
After your refusal
begins the tale of my woes

Which I shall begin from the nails and eye-lashes of the
    basket-weaving girls
who were obliged during a protracted famine
to kill the snow-birds in their baskets

Inclination

Money does not buy death
Death yields itself
Under a droplet of poison
and dark stairs

In quest of death
We wander with those
Whose scaffolds have
no noose to offer us

We search for death in towns
where iron does not rust

Look for it in a cheetah's talons
that have been removed

We buy a place to die
under the shade of a tree
by a monolith
or
in a fickle heart
But we cannot be interred on a bridge

Death does not bar one's way
I do not know why
At the gates of the execution grounds
I was withheld
I do not know how
The dagger auctioneer shall treat me

Why did I make the final bid
When I had
no money to make it good

Perhaps I could borrow from death
A hundred bars of gold
or
Half-a-world
Perhaps I could ask of death
my child
whom a girl is destroying in her womb
into another's womb
to deliver

However
by that time
the shades of night fall on caged beasts
at the far end of the passageway

I am inclined
that I be unfaithful to death

I am inclined
that I tell you
Locked in that dream is my death
That you did not relate

I am inclined
that the dream you bore
I repeat before you
and
fall dead

The Heart of a Poet

Where bounds of love are marked ended
Over the closed door
Regarding the full moon
I made the invocation owed to a rising moon

You chained my heart
And I began to bark

If you so wish
with such a delicate chain
you could tie to the marked tree
a broken branch
that the timber merchant would fell this season

The chained heart
starts to lick your feet
and you said
This dog's reverted
Just as in a tale
a blind man, upon restoration of his sight
had spurned his dog

If you so wish
I could recite to you the poem
that I read
When I used to speak
And was unaware
how many doors away
the gnashing of my teeth could be heard

The poet had said
"My heart is a hound
I am setting it after your scent
You were unfaithful to me
You eloped with another man
My heart will mangle that man's genitals
and your calf in his jaw
drag you back
to me." *

A poet's heart is a hound
And the heart of a chained man
A chained dog

This dog has reverted
It has swallowed its chain
Perhaps your fingers too
That are cold as stone
And unfaithful like this chain
that could tether any dog

* Yehuda Amichai: A Dog after Love

You called the one who cures beasts
And into his eyes, smiling
Decided my fate for me

On the bounds of love, ended
not you
perhaps, somebody else had writ
Whose script
is locked in my heart
like the secret
at which I first learned
to bark

The Dirge of a Rabid Dog

As a laborer
I carried a sack of poison,
from the railway station to the godown
My back was forever stained blue

As a gentleman
I had my back painted white

In the capacity of a farmer
I ploughed an acre of land
My back forever became crooked

As a gentleman
having my spine removed
I had my back straightened

As a teacher
I was made from chalk
A gentleman
from blackboard

As a sexton
I was made from a corpse
As a gentleman
from the spirit of the deceased

In the capacity of a poet
I wrote the dirge of a rabid dog
As a gentleman
I recited it and died

About the Poet

AFZAL AHMED SYED (born 1946 in Ghazipur, India) holds a unique place among contemporary poets of the Urdu language. He is a master of both classical and modern Urdu poetic expression and a leading proponent of linguistic experimentation. He has published three collections of the modern *nazm* genre titled *Chheni Hoi Tareekh* (*An Arrogated Past*, 1984), *Do Zubanon Mein Saza-e Maut* (*Death Sentence in Two Languages*, 1990), and *Rococo Aur Doosri Duniyaen* (*Rococo and Other Worlds*, 2000). He has also published one *ghazal* collection, *Khaima-e Siyah* (*The Dark Pavilion*, 1988). His collected works titled *Matti Ki Kaan* was published in 2009.

About the Translator

MUSHARRAF ALI FAROOQI's critically acclaimed translation of the Indo-Islamic legend *The Adventures of Amir Hamza* was published by Modern Library in 2007. He is currently translating the world's first magical fantasy epic, *Hoshruba* from the Urdu. His novel *The Story of a Widow* (2008) was published by Knopf Canada, and a children's picture book *The Cobbler's Holiday or Why Ants Don't Wear Shoes* (2008) by A Neal Porter Book/ Roaring Brook Press. His website is www.mafarooqi.com.

About The Driftless Series

The Driftless Series is a publication award program established in 2010 and consists of five categories:

DRIFTLESS NATIONAL, for a second poetry book by a United States citizen

DRIFTLESS NEW ENGLAND, for a poetry book by a New England author

DRIFTLESS ENGLISH, for English language poetry from an author outside the United States

DRIFTLESS TRANSLATION, for a translation of poetry into English

DRIFTLESS CONNECTICUT, for an outstanding book in any field by a Connecticut author

The Driftless Series is funded by the Beatrice Fox Auerbach Foundation Fund at the Hartford Foundation for Public Giving. For more information and a complete list of books in The Driftless Series, please visit us online at http://www.wesleyan.edu/wespress/driftless.